Pitiful to Powerful

How to overcome adversity and unlock your greatness!

By Maurice Latham

TABLE OF CONTENTS

DEDICATION

First and foremost I would like to thank my Lord and savior Jesus Christ. I want to dedicate this book to my mother, Nedra Latham and my father, John Wright. Mom you've been here for me through the ups and downs and always reassured me that you would always have my back and my front, you've been nothing short of amazing and for that, I am forever grateful to have you as a mother. To my dad, thank you for accepting me. Although we just met, I feel like I've had you my entire life. Thank you pops. I have no doubt that you would have been there from the start if you knew then, that I was your son.

To all of my supporters thank you. Victoria for loving me even when I made it impossible, thank you baby. To my kids - you are my motivation and you keep me going even when my vision is blurred. Thank you Lawrita for going half with God to create them.

To my brother Jenaurde who I can depend on for anything, I love you bro. My grandma for her prayers and covering. My cousin and mentor Terence Latham, thank you for your advice and support. Coach Emory Addison and the Addison Family, thank you for believing in me when I didn't believe in myself. Coach Buck for helping me navigate fatherhood and for your advice. It helped me out tremendously. Calvin Simon for keeping me grounded spiritually. Coach Kala Dawson for taking a chance on me while I was on the sidelines, thank you. Sean, Tootman, Dion, Kia and my beautiful Aunts Velma and Rita and a handful of supporters I love y'all.

I hope y'all enjoy!

CHAPTER 1: WHO WAS I?

The worst thing that a father can do is remove himself from the equation. It creates a void in not only the family but in every child that man had fathered.

His absence becomes a source of angst, anger, depression, confusion, fear and any number of radical emotions that could creep up on you at a moment's notice. It's a pain that festers deep and relentlessly prods at the hearts and minds of those affected.

The pain is—a cancer in its own right—no "buts" about it. No cure. The hardest thing to face is that life goes on, with or without our tears. I know this all too well. For too many years, I'd lived it with every breath that I took.

Not having my father around left a hole in my life that I'd then tried to fill with a litany of things that would prove only to make my already hard life more difficult. From it, I grew cold and resentful toward him and anything that would so much as remind me of his absence or my own shortcomings, I'd directly attribute to him. I knew I really couldn't blame him for not being there for me. He didn't know he had a son who needed him more than anything in this world. He was in the military and the day my mother found out she was pregnant was the same day he was deployed, and before she knew it, he was gone, and she had no real idea if she would ever see him again. My mom would always tell me good stories about him and swore that if he were here, I would be his right-hand man. That alone kept my hope alive but I still found myself angry at him because I loved him so much.

No matter how I'd tried to filter my anger, the task seemed impossible. I'd held onto my loathing so tightly that it began to manifest in my mood, my attitude, my perception, etc. Literally everything down to the way that I talked, walked and interacted, boiled down to the core belief that, because of not having him, I wasn't good enough.

For years, I'd still found myself waiting for him. My father wasn't around to be the admiral man that I desperately needed in my life or the role model I was seeking in other men. However, he was mine and he was gone. Regardless of his failings, they did nothing to comfort me as I sat on the porch in my neighborhood and envisioned him walking up to me from nowhere, if only to say, "Hey, son. I missed you." That moment never came—at least not when I'd wanted it the most.

Instead of him ascending our porch, I'd wait outside and watch the neighbors' patriarch come home every night and hug his children. Every day he'd come and every day I'd watch—hoping that my father would follow swiftly behind him. Again, that moment never came.

From the first bad bruise, to the first bike ride, to the car accident—where I'd hurt the knee that ultimately ruined my career—my first date, my first heartache and everything else that comprises a young boy's life, I was alone. He missed it all and as far as I could tell, he couldn't have cared less about any of it. My mother would remind me that if he knew I was alive things would be different, but I really couldn't comprehend why my hero wasn't here with me. So in my mind, he couldn't have cared less about me.

All the while, I pictured him sailing across the globe with his new family and not so much as a care in the world about what would become of me. It was the beginning of a lasting anger that would set the course for a large chunk of my life. It was a despise that defined me. It was a despise that I used to defend myself from the world.

Some would come to see me as a martyr of sorts. Others, a guy filled with loads of potential. In my mind, I was neither of those things. I was just a boy who rocked himself to sleep every night while crying out, "I want my dad," between the tears. No matter what I did, no how much time had passed, that boy never went away. Thus, began my journey.

There are so many people who take for granted that they've got both parents at home. A mother who's caring and content. A father who's stern but wise beyond their imagination. Both of them loving, happy, and two parts of a necessary whole...a family.

Those of us, who were selected (and yes, we were selected), to live without that luxury could only dream of such a thing. It isn't a waste of time. In fact, I still think about what that life would have been like—if only to emulate it. It's important to visualize your standards.

I never let myself get too far gone with my fantasies, however. The reality always followed like the drunken headliner after a stellar opening act. Sometimes, I can even count it down. Today, I'll just share it with you openly.

Concerning from where I'd taken my social queues, I'm a bit embarrassed to say that all I'd had to work with were the men around me or the famous ones that I'd happened to catch a glimpse of on television or in movies and other media. Imitation is a compliment to everyone but the imitator.

I, being essentially fatherless, had to take what I could get. I think that it was preferable to the *other* male figure in my life. His name was Gregory. He was a tall, dark-skinned man with a bald head and a voice so deep and raspy that it could narrate the worst of your nightmares.

I don't remember ever specifically being told that he and my mother were married (that's not something that kids ever really hear about.) However, I do recall the moment when I'd read their marriage certificate. At the time, my world had been holding on by a thin shred of hope— provided in the form of my mother. That moment snapped the last remaining bind of my optimism.

It started off cordially enough, I suppose. After that initial bout with dread and fear of change, I was awash with the warm and bitter grasp of possibility. *What if he's what I've been looking for? What if _he_ could be the father that took himself from me?* I'd hoped.

That hope lasted for what now feels like a single second. The longer that Gregory was around, the more I'd found that he was exactly the monster that I feared he would be.

Though, as a deacon, he was lauded by the church; behind closed doors he wrought havoc on my mother, brother, sisters and I. He was an adulterer, to say the least. Every moment that he'd managed to be away from my mother he'd have yet another woman on his arm.

More often than not, it was a member of the church who'd come by under the pretense of seeking council or a prayer. It wasn't long before most of the church had begun whispering rumors and ramblings about Gregory's escapades.

Despite all of that, he still forced us to go to church on Sundays. While he would worship and put on a front while in church, my mother suffered through the hushed voices and spiteful stares of the women her husband had been unfaithful with. My mother stayed just to have a family.

It only worsened over time. Gregory's bad attitude and harsh demeanor inevitably evolved in physical, verbal, and mental abuse—mostly directed at my mother (which was kept quiet) but at times, he'd take a swipe at my brother and I as well for "good measure." Hell is bad but it's so much worse when the devil decides to bunk with you.

He and my mother would bicker and banter all week long about a million things that I was too young to understand. Despite my lack of understanding, I knew one absolute truth—he was treating her badly. Of all the words and lessons that I've learned, that's still the best that I could come up with.

He would leave us alone with no lights, no power...no him. My mother would cry privately. We never saw the tears but a child could sense when their mother wasn't happy. I would sit in silence—angry. My brother would do the same and we would look at each other hopelessly and shake our heads in disappointment and disbelief. All of us were heartbroken and emotionally defeated. Yet, still the best that I could manage to say, "was that he was treating her bad." Some pain never ages. It just rides through life right along with you. I guess that this is a case of that.

By the time that I turned twelve, our domestic chaos had been going on for years. Through some strength outside of herself, my mother found the courage to finally divorce my stepfather and send him packing.

At first, we were happy that the demon's curse had finally been lifted from our home. What kid wouldn't be thrilled to see his bully exiled? However, after a few weeks, I found myself wishing that Gregory would return in almost the same way that I'd wished my father would have come home all those years prior.

It wasn't necessarily for me, nor my brother and sisters, that I'd hoped Gregory would come back. Rather, it was for my mother. As strong-willed and headstrong as she was, she was human. At twelve years old, I'd just realized that for the first time.

I watched as my mother worked tirelessly, day in and day out, just to make sure that we had enough money to be poor. We didn't lack anything, per se, but it was clear by our predicament (and her long shifts at work) that we weren't born with a silver spoon in our mouths, either.

With each day, came a new pain and a worse struggle. With each day, I watched as my mother took it in stride and fought with everything that she had left to keep us satisfied. Suddenly, Gregory's purpose had dawned on me.

What he provided for my mother wasn't just stability and comfort, but a sense of home, completion, and normality (disruptive and miserable as it may have been.) For that, I was guilt-ridden. I wondered if it my fault that Gregory had left. I wondered if it was because of me, that my mother pushed him away.

Day in and day out, she worked. Day in and day out, my own spirit weakened.

Like any marriage built on faith, their separation drove my mother, and my brother my sisters and I away from the church by default. I'm not exactly sure why people feel that when things go wrong, it's okay to blame it on God.

Then again, maybe it wasn't her blaming God. Maybe her view was just tainted. Maybe her broken heart just couldn't bear the memories. Whatever it was, her faith took a serious hit when Gregory left us.

Even though he was gone, something remained. A piece of him. The idea that a man lies. He does it well and he does it frequently. He lies to his wife, his children, his God and worst of all, he lies to himself. It's a lesson that's taken years for me to shake off. I hope that this book can help to spare you some of the wasted time.

CHAPTER 2: WHO I BECAME

As I approached my more formidable high school years, I began to see the sudden manifestations of my trauma. As a child, when you are unfortunate enough to suffer through any type of pain, anguish or event that sticks with you, you tend to develop a personality around it. It's normally nothing too severe but it becomes a definitive characteristic.

Instinctively, as a way of rebuking the painful experience, we develop a sort of scar tissue around our hearts, souls and minds. It's never meant maliciously, but rather to protect us from ever getting hurt in that same way again. You probably have a unique version of this "armor" yourself. It's not uncommon, but there ARE levels of severity to it.

The funny thing about it is that the offended party truly believes that the negative habits that they've developed as a direct result of their trauma, only serves to protect them.

The fact of the matter is that not only do those habits NOT help us, they become a brand new weak spot all on their own and a comically bad mask for the *actual* reasons behind our behavior.

Our "protection" is often the source of our defeat and inner turmoil. Worse yet, most people are completely blind to it. The greatest threat to our success becomes ourselves and our ignorance toward reality.

In the beginning, for me, my "armor" in response to the pain that I'd felt, was lying. I'd been so fed up with my life and all of the horrible things that had happened to me, that I'd convinced myself that the only way to survive it was to ignore it completely. Even if I couldn't do that, I figured that if I could convince others of my lies, *it would bandage the wound all the same*.

I found myself lying to my classmates and people I didn't know to cover the pain and present the enhanced image I had of myself to seem more than what I'd appeared to be. I lied to my teachers to get out of trouble (that I deserved to be in) when cheating on exams. Things around me were so bad that I would lie to myself in hopes of my lie becoming the truth. I was so tired of not knowing who I was. As a teenager, what I didn't realize right away, was that those lies weren't helping me. The lies were detaching me from reality and sending me on a path so far away from where I should have been, that eventually, I lost myself in it.

From my protection (my armor) a problem was birthed that would come to redefine my entire existence. I would no longer know who I was. I gave up my identity just so that I would no longer have to deal with the pain of having one.

Being as lost as I was then, it felt right. Only honesty with myself could set me straight. I wouldn't discover that until much later. But let me not get too far ahead of myself.

With all of the nightmarish days and harsh realities that my family was faced with, my mother still tried her best to provide for my brother and my siblings. As you could probably imagine, life after the divorce was hard.

With my brother and I both too young to hold legal jobs, my mother was forced to take on the weight of the five of us all by herself. I'm still completely taken aback by how strong and willing she was to carry the load of an entire family. How she refused to give up on herself or us. Even on her hardest day, she would be ready to take on the world just to provide for us.

Whether she meant to or not, her struggle planted a seed in my mind. It informed me that with enough fight and enough drive, you can conquer any hardship—so long as you don't stray from your resolve to press on in the face of that which threatens to take you down.

I'd like to believe that it's from her that I'd eventually derived my own strength. You don't bear witness to something like that and walk away with nothing, even if you want to.

In addition to everything that my mother did, she also went above and beyond to make sure that although she was gone a lot—with a variety of jobs—she still loved us very much and held us dearly in her broken heart.

She'd prop up our egos with encouraging declarations like we're "smart," "strong," and "leaders," among other amazing attributes. She gave us as much love as she knew how. No one ever taught her how to love, so she was doing the best that she could. It's sad to admit but it just wasn't enough. The wound that Gregory left was too big for one quick fix.

A house is never really the same once you remove a brick from its foundation. Hate him or not, Gregory's departure rippled through all of our lives like a raging tide—devastating and merciless.

There I was, just a kid looking out for himself and coming up empty-handed. Even with my mother's love, my longing for an identity grew. I wanted something more. Something new. Something that was like me. As some kids do, I found it in the streets.

The "dope-boys" were like the celebrities of my neighborhood. Whereas an adult could easily see through the false *machismo* and "gangsta" bravado, as a teen, I was enthralled by it.

There was something that just seemed special about having the nice clothes, the jewelry, the cars, the notoriety. Meanwhile, my brother, my sisters and I were walking around with holes in our clothes and near empty stomachs.

In my mind, they were success incarnate. Right there in front of me, I began to sway toward it. Luckily for me, my mother was there to intervene before things had gone too far. I'd nearly worked up the nerve to dive into that life. It looked lavish and filled with promise.

One day, after one of my mother's worst weeks, I'd told her about my newfound aspirations.

She could hear it in my voice that it was something that that sparked my interest. I tried to goad her on with the fantasies of "living the life" and finally being at peace and comfortable.

When she asked me, gently (as was her way), where I'd gotten that crazy idea from, I told her about a dope-boy that I'd seen every day on my way to school. He was my age, with his own car, a beautiful woman and a thick gold chain that dangled down his chest. I told her that I wanted to have the things he had and be "rich and carefree."

Her answer was short but succinct and purposeful. "He'll be dead or in jail before graduation," she said. "I want better things for you, Maurice." I took pause after she'd said that. My mother was loving and sometimes stern but I'd never heard her speak quite so confidently about the downfall of another person—a kid, at that.

The next day, when I went to school, I just walked past him. No admiration. No urge to converse. Not so much as a hint of jealousy. "He'll be dead or in jail," her voice sang through my head like a negro spiritual. It kept me sane when I'd been so willing to jump ship into a life of crime.

Sure enough, two weeks later, that same kid was dead. Gunned down in cold blood by a local rival. That cluster of events quickly ended my druglord dreams. It changed how I saw things for the better. It was one of the few lessons that was actually able to cut through my hard head. I'm glad that it did.

Despite the close call with the corners, I found myself in the same predicament. Alongside my hunger for glory and money, I'd still been lost and looking for direction. I was still looking for me.

I was forced to search for my path elsewhere. At the very least, I wanted to find a direction to lead me to something that I could follow. What I found, was basketball.

I was never necessarily a huge fan of the game. To be honest, I could have taken it or left it wherever it may have crossed my path. In my HOOD, basketball was one of the of the ways to escape poverty (especially for broke kids.) I got tired of seeing my mother struggle and I made up my mind that I would die trying to perfect my craft so I could take care of her. The game was complex enough to keep my mind occupied, physically demanding enough that nothing would ever come easy, and above all else, it was fair. Only the strong survived and only those who worked like hell would ever find any modicum of success. Those things appealed to me. *"Finally,"* I thought, *"Something that I can control."*

Despite my commitment to the game, my first year I was cut from the team. It was my first real brush with failure. It was a failure that I couldn't attribute to anything but my own inadequacy. I couldn't blame anyone but myself, and for that I hated me.

I beat myself up. I told myself that I would get revenge. That inner voice emerged, and I decided that the coach was at fault.

For the first time in my life, I'd had an enemy with a face that I could seek vengeance on. I didn't want to do anything malicious (though the thoughts warmed my insides.)

I knew that any harmful recourse would only lead me to worse things. However, *I could prove him wrong. I could push myself.* "I CAN BEAT HIM," I thought. It was an odd mix of good impulses and bad direction. In either case, my drive carried me off the court that day.

I specifically remember the walk home afterward. Mom was constantly at work (bless her heart) so I'd often have to "hoof it" back and forth to school. That day, I had a grumble in my stomach—a result of my over-stressing about being cut from the team.

Needless to say, I wished that I didn't have to walk. I would have much rather been rushed home so that I could sulk in silence and mope. Lucky for me, I'm not that lucky. That walk gave me a chance to clear my head and gave me my first glimpse of "self."

I told myself that "this will never happen again." I resolved to it. Chanted it. Shouted it at the streets, "Never again!" Then, just like that, I was home, and "myself" evaporated into the same thing that it'd always been. A question. "But how?"

That night, I waited up for my mother to come home. I was filled questions that demanded answers I couldn't provide for myself. At around three in the morning, she'd strolled in—looking tired. She was always tired.

Before she'd arrived, I'd practiced my "I got cut" script over and over in my head a million times, until it was *just* right. I could damn near say it backwards. At the sound of her footsteps, I raced to downstairs to blurt out my lines. Then, I saw hers. The bags under eyes. The wrinkles of her drained smile. Her shaky legs that needed sleep.

I stopped in my tracks. I forgot my lines. All I could do was listen to the sound of my mother's voice in my head telling me to "be strong." For the first time in, God knows how long, I listened to her—even though she hadn't said a word.

I gave her a hug and asked her how her night was. I didn't see the point in bringing up what had happened with the team. She'd had enough on her plate and didn't need to hear my "drama." Instead, I just spoke to her for a while.

At some point, talk of my birthday came up in the discussion. When she asked me what I wanted, I just answered, "Ankle weights." She got them for me. I put them on and practically never took them off. They were every bit a part of my wardrobe as socks and underwear. My armor and my answer to defeat.

That summer, I woke every day at six in the morning. I would get dressed, brush my teeth, eat, strap on my ankle weights and walk to the nearest basketball court—four miles away. As I practiced, I would envision every single member of the team was guarding me at once. Every dribble, every shot, every juke and every move was against them. I wouldn't stop until my legs were ready to collapse beneath me.

Afterward, I would walk back home with no water. Sometimes, I'd be fortunate enough to bring along some celery and peanut butter. I would get home, rest for a few hours and then head right back to the basketball court. I'd work out and return home, rest, then go back later that night.

It was like clockwork and I was the main gear—spinning endlessly, passionately, unstoppably. Little did I know, I was developing my work ethic. The same one that I use today—albeit for all the wrong reasons. "Never again," I'd tell myself. Before I knew it, summer was over and I was back at school raring to go.

On the day that tryouts had rolled around, I was walking the halls with the star point guard, Terrence James. Word around town was that he was the best basketball player that they'd ever seen. I didn't buy into much of the hype until I saw it for myself.

To my surprise, the rumors were true. The first time that I'd ever seen him play, I was floored. He could dribble like Allen Iverson, shoot like Ray Allen, and had the tireless kind of play that rivaled Kobe Bryant.

Once, I'd seen him do a move called the *'shamgod'* on a guy (*a move where you throw the ball out in front of the opponent in hopes of him grabbing for it and as soon as he reach for it you pull it back leaving him off balance and embarrassed.)* The guy on the other side of the ball fell to his knees in embarrassment, then flat on his STOMACH and didn't get up until the play was over. Terrence was an all-around true point guard. On top of all of that, he'd seemed to know himself. Even a guy like me could admire that about a person.

He made a comment as we walked into the gym, jokingly saying, "Let's see who is about to get cut." I knew that was directed at me, but he had no idea of the work that I'd put in that summer.

There were no weaknesses in my game. My crossovers were crisp. My spin moves were tight. My dunks could shatter a backboard. I had everything. All I needed was the chance to show the world (my little world) just how much I'd improved. Boy, did I show them.

From the second that I hit the court—to the last step I took off it—I was the only thing worth watching. I was their king. I'd fought for my crown and was now ready to accept the genuflects from my people.

After the first day of tryouts, the coach (Cornel Parker) who'd cut me the previous year, asked who I was. I immediately said to him, "You cut me last year." He smiled and responded, "I did?" I was always told I was a great ball player but never had that confirmation. I was bottled-up potential, full of greatness but I wasn't molded. I wasn't ready.

Walking home one day, a kid (probably around thirteen or fourteen) stopped me. He told me that he was playing with his friends at the playground and he was imitating the way I played and was dominating his friends.

I didn't understand the magnitude of what he'd said back then because the belief in myself was nonexistent. I knew I'd put in the work but I didn't know how good I really was. Peggy O'Mara said it best when she said, "The way we talk to our kids becomes their inner voice." All that I could hear was the emptiness inside of myself. It was loud and it was numbing.

That emptiness gave way for my insecurity to flourish once more. With one success in my pocket, I returned to my original failure. I wanted guidance. I wanted a father. I craved it more than any dunk, dribble or shot. I craved it more than any victory. I craved it more than air. A man's approval. A man's word. A man's direction.

By that point in my life, I'd never really had a man tell me how to be a man. I didn't know where I stood. I didn't know what I was worth. Because of that, I sought high and low to find someone who could show me the path. I'd hoped that I could mean something to them as well. Whatever male figure came to me with advice about my game, I'd listen to like a brainwashed soldier; even if it hurt me.

I was given the nickname "BEAST" by teammates because of the way I played. A lot of my intense play was the result of built-up anger. I told myself that it was all just because *I felt* abandoned by my father. I figured that if I'd worked like crazy and made it into the NBA, "That'll show him. That'll be a sweet revenge."

Truth is, it wouldn't have mattered if I'd made it into the big leagues or not. It wouldn't have even mattered if my father came back that very day and swore to stick by my side. Nope. By then, the damage was done. The problem was bigger than just someone leaving me. The problem *was* me.

Even though I'd worked my ass off, made the team and found a modicum of success, I couldn't register it. I didn't see it. My teammates called me "beast." Inside, I didn't feel like one. I didn't go by that name in my own head. My crazy mind preferred things like "stupid," "ugly," and "weak." A broken spirit starts with the heart and works inward. I didn't know how to fix that.

I remember my coach, Cornel Parker, telling me before a game, "I believe you can play in the NBA." That night, I went out and dominated both ends of the floor. That one affirmation gave me everything I needed. *"Imagine what I could have been like having been told these things from birth,"* I thought.

Another night before a game, my uncle jokingly called me a weak ball player and that I was garbage. Like a wicked specter, that unstable inner voice that I created went to work. It ate at me. It ate at my game. I became that weak player. After one of the worst hours of my life—the worst game of my life—I got home and just curled up in a ball on my bed.

I couldn't sleep, so I went to the basketball court and proceeded to destructively tear myself down while working hard on my game. I was either too young or too hurt to face the facts. My game wasn't the problem. My way of thinking was. My lack of faith was.

After the season ended and after winning eastern district player of the year, I went off to college with no identity, no male structure, a foundation fostered by a weary mother and a large empty sack of "what nows?" My mother had done the best that she could but I learned then, what I know now. That old saying is true. "A woman can't raise a boy to be a man." No offense intended. I'm just sharing my thoughts on the matter.

So, there I was. Angry, afraid, confused, slighted; on a plane and getting ready to part ways with the one person on God's green earth who had ever selflessly given of herself to help me be better.

When I said "goodbye" to my mother that day, I had a big chip on my shoulder to prove to everyone whom I'd ever seen treat my mother and I wrong. It was the first day of the rest of my life. It was the first time that it actually hit me. I was going to be alone. Me and all of my confusion. Still no identity. Still no direction. Leaving my only support behind.

"Any boy who does not have confirmation of who he is will eventually make mistakes as a man until he finds himself."

CHAPTER 3: "LET GO, TO GROW."

When a child is raised with no identity, they are sure to make mistakes as an adult.

The only way to guarantee growth is to learn from those mistakes and keep moving forward. Never mind the fear or regret of your past follies and foibles. Break away from the failure that you've seen and the habits that you've mimicked.

Reach for the barriers and DESTROY THEM. Fly as high as you can with a single-minded focus on ascending further. DROP THE DEAD WEIGHT.

I know, it sounds crazy. You're thinking, "But Maurice, I'm different. I can't be saved." I'll spare you the "everyone is special" speech and cut to the chase. Yes, you are different but you are not undiagnosable.

You suffer from a human condition; an emotional one at that. I don't need a lab coat and some goggles to tell you that you have low self-esteem that is bred from your years of seeking an identity only to become the result of your negative inner voice.

You've become a person that your negative inner voice has tricked you into becoming and you're not happy about it. You're downright pissed off—as you should be. That emotion is a sign. It means that you're ready to do something about it.

Though my story may be different from yours (quite likely), if not for anything else, our troubles are rooted together in that void and negative inner voice. Think of it as a disease. It attacks everyone the same. In this particular case, the disease is insecurity and self-doubt. It doesn't matter how you've contracted it. The fact is that you've got it.

It's hard to accept and even harder to hear. But, you can never solve a problem until you admit that it exists. You MUST face the reality of who you are, if only to keep that darkness from swallowing you whole.

If you don't take the action NOW, at the end of the day all that you'll be left with is negative self-talk like:

"You aren't good enough."

"Your parents didn't do it, you can't" either."

"You are ugly."

"You aren't smart enough."

...and a bunch of other crazy ideas, that you should *NEVER* listen to. In the end, you are your thoughts. In the end, you control your thoughts. By proxy, that means that YOU CONTROL YOU.

Even those of us who find our way into various levels of accomplishment and positivity are ravaged by that inner voice. It reminds us of our mistakes and our wrongdoings. It rips us up from the inside out. It wriggles its way into our lives and slowly chops away at all the good that we've got until we're nothing but what it says we are (stupid, dumb, crazy, foolish, etc.)

In some of the worst cases I've heard, it's even caused people to hurt themselves and others to kill themselves.

When this voice is not defeated, you settle for what life gives you. You don't try to improve. You blame everyone else. You become angry at the people who chased their dreams and made it. You stop caring how you look physically because you feel you have nothing to live for.

If you let this voice define you, you will find yourself looking for validation from someone else to make you feel better about you. DON'T LISTEN TO IT! FOCUS!

If you don't control that inner voice and that negative self-talk, there will continue to be mistakes made. Left unchecked, one day you may make the ultimate one. At best, if you do nothing, you'll simply be stuck in a cycle of chaos and confusion while you trip through the minefields of life—making mistake after mistake until you are so far away from success that you can barely even spell it.

Shut down that inner voice! Exile the negative self-talk! Free yourself from yourself! Most of all, forgive yourself and always look for the lesson.

Seeking Growth

When I was in college, I still had no clue who I was. I had problems making and maintaining friendships with my peers. If I wasn't pushing them away with my own special brand of "fuck-off," I was sending physical signals to ensure they knew not to test me.

If it was a fight they'd wanted, I was willing to bring it to their front door. Everything even slightly more positive than that, I wouldn't trust. I would treat them like they were the disease, while at the same time being completely ignorant to the *real* sickness in my life.

They weren't the problem. My own thoughts and perception were my problem. They drove me to a degree of isolation that no person should be forced to endure (self-imposed or otherwise.) I was a little more forgiving with women. With men, however, I was merciless in my disgust and rejection of them.

In my mind, they were nothing but younger versions of my father and projections of the ongoing nightmare that I'd been living in. I was fearful of what may have happened if they'd gotten too close. Instead of allowing myself to be vulnerable, I made sure they feared me just as much as I'd feared that platonic intimacy.

A boy's first "guy friend" is usually his father. I never had that, so I created this strong dislike for men, because in my mind every man was out to hurt me (just like my father.) No matter how friendly, how giving, or how sincere they were, I just couldn't bring myself to trust them. To me, they were all the enemy. They were just like the guys I'd envisioned on the court the previous summer. They were something that I needed to conquer and defeat.

My brother and I came up with this is motto that we both started to live by:

> **"Keep people at a distance and destroy every man physically."**

I took that attitude with me to college. At times, it worked in my favor—primarily on the basketball court. For the most part, however, all it did was serve to further alienate me from building any meaningful bonds with my brothers-in-arms. Not every man is a saint but not every man is sinner. I damned them all. For my prejudice, I'd unknowingly damned myself.

If a guy wanted to "hang," or "chill," or whatever else that friends do, I took it as an immediate threat. I'd always assumed that their intentions were to hurt or otherwise harm me in some way, shape or form. For that, I resented them, and I rebuked them.

I found the issue less severe with women. Though, I was cautious with them as well, I would take what I could from whomever seemed useful but for the most part, I stuck to my guns and kept to myself. You might have seen a smile but you'd never seen me. It's hard to live that way. I'd abandoned myself, not realizing that I was just doing what I thought my father had done to me. I was living in the wound and hadn't the slightest clue that I was.

My life wasn't all cloak and dagger, however. I'd still managed to take some lessons from male influencers who (I tried to believe) cared. Most of the time they were older. Just old enough for me to let my guard down a bit and be "parented."

My college coaches, Coach Laing and Coach Buck had wives and families, and the moment I saw how they were very family-oriented, I knew I wanted to be that kind of guy. I started watching them closely; how they treated their kids and wives and they gave me my first image of how a married man should behave.

I saw how they ate dinner as a family and enjoyed each other's company with little room for arguments. I watched how they respected their wives and kept their kids in line with a loving grip.

I actually witnessed something that I'd only been able to imagine prior to being there. I saw peace.

There were no shrouds, no lies, no fronts. It was just a family—together and happy. Even though I was still lost, I knew then, that I wanted one of my own. I wanted a foundation built on that mutual appreciation and absolute love and affection. I wanted to be them. I wanted to build that for myself. I still had a way to go before I'd get it for myself.

I was twenty and confused and still seeking confirmation and acceptance. I began to seek sex as a temporary cover. I wasn't addicted but when that inner voice began to remind me that I was a wandering generality (a boy with no plan as to who he is or where he's going.) I used women and sex to escape because that made me feel like a man.

I knew that a man was supposed to treat woman right but I'd never seen a man be faithful. All that I could remember was my mom working two jobs and her husband gallivanting around the house with some strange woman when she wasn't home.

I knew something was wrong and I confirmed it when I randomly looked out of the window one day after my stepfather and this lady (whose name I never knew) left our home and held hands as they walked down the street. I now know that it was something small but at the time, it was an epiphany—a defining moment of my upbringing. That day, it became "okay" to be unfaithful.

In the early years of my life, I'd made so many mistakes. Just like you, I didn't even realize that I was making most of them. My lack of perception was key in the ongoing chain that nearly broke me.

Now, years older and (hopefully) wiser, I can tell you that there is a way to escape that dark hole.

Understand that it is possible to rebound from any mistake or situation. Know that all that is required of you is that you be willing to acknowledge that you've made them and be open to facing them, even if it hurts. ESPECIALLY if it hurts. We must learn to navigate through our shortcomings.

The first thing you must do is let go of your mistake and the emotion but don't forget the lesson. Don't hold grudges with yourself about something that has already been done. No more beating yourself up. You won't ever be perfect, so stop trying to be. Those tragedies are just shaping the stronger and better YOU. Don't get caught up in your history. You're not the mistakes of your past—you've actually gained from mistakes— especially if you've learned from them. No more putting yourself in a box of guilt and depression.

You are phenomenal in your mistakes. Mistakes are just a moment of lapsed judgment. Learn from them. Grow from them. Avoid repeating them. Even if you do repeat, learn from that and fight like hell to grow.

It's not over until you win. You can use that mistake as your best friend or your worst enemy. A friend will help you learn from the mistake and apply it to your life to help you grow. An enemy will remind you of that mistake and leave you to dwell in the abyss of your misjudgment. Be mindful of your thoughts and be fair to yourself. There's no need to beat yourself up about anything. The world has enough bullies up to that task. THE JOB IS FILLED! STOP APPLYING FOR IT!

"Learn to thrive through your mistakes."

I had to use my mistakes to learn my lessons and to help me to become the man I desperately wanted to become. After I grew and started to become the man I wanted to be, I contacted and called all the people I hurt on my journey and apologized. But it wasn't for them. I did it for me. I did it because I had to *let go, to grow*.

Don't define yourself based on your mistakes, let them nurture you. I'm not saying go out and do things that you know are wrong, I'm saying that on your journey to becoming the person God created you to be, you will make wrong turns. It's inevitable. Sometimes when making a wrong turn, you find something you never knew existed. When it happens, use it for your own good. This is when it's okay to have amnesia. Make the mistake, learn the lesson and forget the details.

Without mistakes, you can't grow and without growth, you can't become the person who you were created to be. If you can't become who you were created to be, you can't be happy. If you can't be happy, then you are slowly walking to an early grave. The person who hasn't made any mistakes hasn't done anything spectacular.

It's as simple as that.

CHAPTER 4: LOOKING FOR APPROVAL

When a man or a woman continually struggles with "who they are" or "who they're meant to be," the search for approval becomes a drug.

With the rise of social media and the subsequent societal shift it's caused, it's easier to receive the desired and distorted approval of others. At the same time, it also makes it difficult for a person to find out who they are. Individuals are becoming so afraid of their own thoughts and doubtful of their own opinions, that they lose themselves in the digital sewage system that is their timeline and the drain of their notifications.

Social media is now used as a fantasyland where people who have the lowest self-esteem allow relative strangers to define who they are. Their self-confidence is a complete gamble and how they are feeling from minute-to-minute is dictated by how many "likes" they receive or comments get thrown their way.

Some people will even post their darkest secrets to get the opinion of a stranger rather than praying to their creator and trusting their own instincts. Seeking approval from a veritable focus group of random folks IS NOT how you get things done. Networking is fine but crowdsourcing your livelihood is one of the most haphazard things that you could ever do. Why leave your identity to chance?

I cannot overemphasize how important it is that you find out who you are and what you are. Instead of "scrolling for sympathy," spend as much time as possible developing YOU as a person; whether it's reading books, going to seminars, spending time with yourself away from relationships, etc.

If you are a single man or woman, seek out *real* advice from people who you genuinely look up to. I don't mean people with the money or the fame. I mean people with the quality and love of life who don't mind sharing their secrets with you. Seek these people out like a hunter in the wild. Learn from them. Grow from them.

One thing that really helped me out was asking a handful of people who I really admired, to express their views of me. I asked them to write them on a piece of paper or text them to me. It was a daunting thing to put myself through and a humbling thing to ask of people—especially ones who you respect.

Ultimately, I know that I had to do it for my own good. Honesty is unbiased to emotion or feelings. It's the stone-cold truth—cut and dried. It was nerve-racking, for sure. But from these people, I knew that it would be nothing but information that would enlighten, educate and provide perspective to me before my sick inner voice took the wheel and drove me into a wall.

It may seem as if I was looking for approval, but the comments only confirmed what I already knew about who I was as a person. I stuck with it and built myself and my standard from that point.

"Find people that you trust and plead for their honesty."

You can do everything that I mentioned above. I'd recommend it. This is what I discovered, and I believe you will, too: Even if you have the most inspirational people in the world tell you who you are and what you are, only you can truly define your identity. Who you are is up to YOU and no one else. Whether you know it or not, it's always been that way.

How you view and treat yourself is how the world will view and treat you. It's okay to look for guidance from other people but don't look for answers. You must do the work to get the answers.

I was always told that I was a good basketball player. I remember playing against Florida Atlantic University where the former coach, Matt Dougherty (of the North Carolina Tar Heels) had been the head of an all-star team.

I scorched his team (26 points and 14 rebounds) playing my (then legendary) tough game. When that final buzzer sounded and the game had ended, Matt Dougherty found me on the court and whispered in my ear, "You're going to make a ton of money playing this game one day, kid."

I knew that I was good but I had no idea I was worthy of that compliment, so I began looking at my game from those kind words and silenced that small negative voice in my head. I stopped being so hard on myself and started believing in my own ability.

I now understand that some people have a way of seeing the greatness inside of you—even when you don't—and sometimes, all that it takes is one confirmation to temporarily fill that gap. Matt Dougherty gave me that confirmation and that's the first time I really believed I was capable of playing professional basketball. BUT, it took ME to make that call. I had to decide that Coach Dougherty was right. I had to approve of ME.

I had to understand that it was okay to be the best at what I did rather than to minimize my skills to appease others. I had to tell myself that it was okay not to know everything and the things I didn't know were safe to ask about. I had to humble myself where necessary and be proud when I'd earned it. I had to be my own critic. Good or bad, I had to learn to be fair to myself.

You have to know that you are smart. **SAY IT UNTIL YOU BELIEVE IT**. Read and research everything to expand your mind. It takes daily work but it's worth it. Know your value. Accept your faults.

Be willing to find what you love and chase it down with everything you've got. It's okay to scream and rant and rave. Your passion SHOULD make you do that. Don't allow the negative people a word in edgewise. YOU are your judge. It's your job; no one else's.

NOW is the time to stop looking for approval from other people who are also looking for approval from others. Don't live a life waiting for the validation of someone else to make you happy. The only approval you need is the approval of yourself.

Speak to the king or queen inside you immediately. Feel good today. Don't let anybody immobilize you by looking for approval. It's okay to believe that you are the best, the most beautiful, the smartest, the most handsome, the boss, the greatest. No one can take that from you but you and no one else can make you feel less than that. Don't make the opinions of others more important than your own. What others think of you is not important but what you think about yourself is ultimately the deciding factor of your happiness. Build a life that has no ceilings and no limits. The only limits are the ones you put on yourself.

Don't be the kind of person who gives attention and time to what people say or think about you to be happy. Don't give your power away to someone else in the form of approval- seeking and telling yourself that you must have their approval. Who you are is what you think about.

When you are looking for approval, you are completely shutting down your self-importance and literally telling yourself, "What I think of me is irrelevant and what they think of me is the truth." What people say about you is just their opinion; only you have the power to make their opinion a fact.

The good thing about life is you can become what you think without the permission of others. Check your thoughts daily. Decide what you want with your life and who you want to become and become that person mentally. Work like hell every day to become who you want to be.

If I want to become a man of integrity, I will first tell myself every day that I am an integrity-filled man (regardless of my past.) I will take steps toward becoming that man. Man or woman, you can, too. Start by setting small goals for yourself, like going the entire day without telling a lie, keeping your word for the week or even fulfilling an overdue promise. Start small and build massive. You'll get there.

Research (courtesy of *The Huffington Post*) shows that it takes twenty-one days of doing something for it to become a habit. Go twenty-one days (504 hours) without seeking the approval of others. Use this time to practice your positive self-talk and strengthen your own self-image. Rebuild yourself as your greatest self.

Every day for the next twenty-one days, repeat this phrase and watch as you begin to see a dramatic change inside and outside of yourself.

"I am unbelievably powerful. I am grateful for my life today. I chose to love me, despite the failures or mistakes I made yesterday. I am smart, intelligent and I am the best at what I do. I don't need anyone's approval to confirm my decisions for my beautiful life. My opinion of myself is more important than your opinion of me. I am phenomenal! Other people's opinion of me is not my reality. I am my reality."

—Maurice Latham

CHAPTER 5: A PROCESS REVEALED THE REAL ME

There will be times in your life where it will seem as if everything is working and all of your hard work has paid off. This is a sign that you have excelled and entered in to a new level of life. This is the time where you should stop for a second and enjoy your successes. But...never stop your development and personal growth, because after the excitement fades, there will be another demon to challenge you at this new level.

Understand that successful people aren't exempt from the stresses of life. When you finally decide what you want for your life and take action, that's when life will throw boulders—big and small—to discourage you from reaching your goals. This is called *the process*.

The process is designed to make you quit and doubt yourself. Within the process, is that small negative self-talk. In the process, procrastination is magnified. It is in the process, where fear devours dreams but it is also in the process, where the real you is created.

I believe that we are created in shells. Inside that shell is this powerful version of ourselves, who possesses everything that we need and everything that we'd ever wanted. The more we challenge our fears, the more we get up after falls and failures, the more we do the things that make us better (such as going to seminars, reading books, taking classes, etc.), the more that we peel off our shells, then the closer we become to revealing the person we were created to be. This is a journey that has to be enjoyed even when it's not enjoyable and you must keep in mind that these things are not happening *to* you, they are happening *for* you.

I look at life as the stubborn bully, this selfish dictator.

Life doesn't care who you are or what you want. Life doesn't care about how hard you work or what you've been through. All that life is concerned about is continuing the cycle of "winners and losers" with no partiality for which category you fall into.

I know that sounds scary BUT, the thing about life is that it is uncaring. Because of that, you can beat life into submission and mold it into whatever it is that you want it to be. As aloof as life is to the wants, needs and desires of the people in it, it is FORCED to pay attention when those brave enough (the successful people) dare to bang on its door and DEMAND that it bend to their will. Again, that takes practice. It takes heart. It takes perseverance.

"Life is not a fighter,
but a master manipulator."

... it will try to take you down at your weakest ... when you're most comfortable or relaxed in your resolve. Stay on the ball once you've gotten on it and be prepared for life's manipulation. It may come in the form of financial, emotional, physical or familial distractions. PAY ATTENTION and defend yourself and your dreams with EVERYTHING that you've got.

It amazes me how there are so many people who just accept what life is gives them. Life is selfish, so it will give you the bare minimum if you don't show life who's the boss.

Every day should be used as an opportunity to tap into your greatness. Don't let your dream become stagnant. No more fear of failing. In fact, the more failure you face and learn to overcome, the more successful you will be.

Let me explain. History has shown that every great and successful person didn't just become successful the first time they decided to chase a dream.

Every successful person has failed in some way, shape, or form before they'd arrived. No matter the severity of the loss, they take it in good candor. That is because they understand that they are actually growing and *becoming who they were created to be*. There's no progress if there's no risk and failure.

They aren't merely taking a loss; they're learning which ways to win. They're tightening up their strategy and sharpening their skills. For them, every loss is a step closer to victory.

I understood that and I took the leap of faith. I started to do things to change my life and my circumstances. I also understood that the day I made up my mind to chase my dream, that I was going to be faced with some failures and some setbacks. In the face of it all, I kept on. It was never easy. It never will be.

Let me tell you, I've been called all types of things in the last few years. Some may even call themselves "exposing me." But, the journey I had to endure, from a suffering a knee injury that ended my basketball career to working as a housekeeper after being a professional basketball player and EKGs being performed on my heart twice. From sleeping in a room where it was infested with mildew and fleas and a had hole in the ceiling where rain would flood the room if I didn't put pots and buckets down to catch the water to asking my then-wife for a divorce and tearing my family completely apart. From having to sleep on my mother's floor in her small home so my kids could sleep on the available bed and battling a sleeping pill addiction to bullets riddling through my car while driving. From protecting my family with the law working against me and not for me, to leaving me faced with three possible felonies. From having a 465 credit score at the age of 31, foraging for loose change in my car to buy something to eat, being unemployed and owing the IRS thousands of dollars, to resting in my storage unit where I was surrounded by everything I ever worked for. I've been THROUGH HELL.

So, trust me, I understand your pain...

BUT, I made it out. I made it out by embracing that fear. I made it out by accepting my trials and rising to the occasion. I made it out by admitting my mistakes and doing everything in my power to prevent myself from making them again.

I took those failures and turned them into lessons that taught me more with every day that I lived committed to success. I threw away my notions of being "lucky," "fortunate" or "born with a silver spoon." It was TIME TO STOP PLAYING AROUND WITH LIFE AND GET TO WORK!

Right now, you may be experiencing some trying times in your life. This is the perfect opportunity to challenge your inner greatness. Welcome this pain. Welcome the trials and the fact that you will fail when chasing your dream. I know that's terrifying to you but do it anyway. FACE THAT FEAR! CHASE SUCCESS!

Every successful person I've encountered had one major thing in common—the way that they think. They don't doubt. They think about the possibilities. They don't bask in negativity. They think positive thoughts.

Successful people don't worry about what the next man or woman is doing. They think, "How could I make this the best that I can for me?" They leap forth into opportunity without fear, without hate, without anything but their belief that they can SUCCEED! Why can't that be you? Why not start right now?

Successful people look at failure as a life lesson rather than an actual failure. Failure just eliminates your weaknesses, so never stop trying and taking risks after you've been tested because life will bow down to you and give you your dreams.

The more you push and run from pain (and for sure failure), the more persistent it will become. Welcome those hard times; there are lessons to be learned and experiences to be gained. Start looking at trying times with some excitement. NO, it's not fun in *the process* but if you change the way you think in the midst of a trial, you will be amazed at how much you will learn and how much stronger you will become.

Some people, who don't understand, will use the phrase, "It's easier said than done." I say, "It's easier to do if you watch what you say." What you say will eventually manifest. If you say, "It's easier said than done," guess what? It will be easier said than done. WATCH YOUR WORDS!

I'm a firm believer in Christ and his words; the only word that's accurate (in my humble opinion.) Even if you subscribe to another religion, I'd suggest a reading of *The King James Bible*—if for nothing else—than the wisdom that has survived literally thousands of years.

I remember after my separation, a great friend of mine, Timeca Addison, bought me a bible and she told me to get to reading. I started with the Book of Proverbs and I immediately started applying in to my life. This book and the Book of Matthew became a guiding factor of my life and the cornerstone for my belief system—both in and out of the church.

For instance, in Matthew 15: Verse 19, Jesus said,

"But what comes out of the mouth gets its start in the heart. It's from the heart that we vomit up evil arguments, murders, adulteries, fornication, thefts, lies and cussing."

It's the message.

My message.

The same one that I'm teaching you now.

The same thing applies to your success and dreams as it does for your mind, body and soul.

You won't be perfect in this, so be gentle with yourself, develop compassion towards yourself despite your failures, setbacks and mistakes.

I'm not simply spewing some jargon to help you "get rich" or "famous." I'm trying to help you live a life that you could look back on with a smile and use as an example for others. I'm trying to help you find a way back to being whole and happy. I'm giving you a way out of stagnancy.

There were times where my dreams and goals seemed to be stagnant. It's a sign that you've learned what you needed to get to that stage of your life. Now, it's time for a new level in your life —

but like most people —you savor some success, you get comfortable and you stop there. NEVER stop trying new things and taking risks. Trial and error will propel you to your new level and closer to your destination every time, without fail.

Enjoy the process and discover your strength. Even when you aren't seeing the results you're seeking, don't focus on what you don't have; that is the time to strengthen your focus and meditate on what you want. Follow those thoughts into action.

That's success.

The process consists of having faith and faith is a gift and a test. When you finally say "yes" to your dreams and your goals, that faith will be tested. There will be trials and tribulations but enjoy this time of your life. Take chances and go for what you want. Risk failing at something you love versus failing at something you don't.

CHAPTER 6: DIVORCE THE OTHER YOU

In my years of living, I've noticed that the longer I remain the same, the further out of reach my dreams became. I don't care how much you visualize and think about something you want in your life. If you don't change who you are and divorce the old you—regardless of whether or not you receive that dream or gift—you will not be prepared for it and you will lose it. You don't get what you deserve, you get what you are.

Look at it this way. In divorce, for the most part, people go through hell. You've already lost your spouse and on top of that you may even lose your home or car and be left with your finances in shambles. It's a harrowing experience.

In this divorce (the divorce of yourself), you stand to lose nothing but the things that have held you back. I know that it sounds nice and flowery, but you'd be surprised how difficult it is to part ways with the habits that have kept you alive.

Yes, maybe that thing you do (that you shouldn't) keeps you afloat. But, I ask you, do you just want to float above water? Do you simply want to wade in a dying pool of your repetitive mistakes? Or, do you want to rise above them and fly? Make your choice wisely and commit to it. Just know three things:

1.) It's going to hurt A LOT and that's okay.
2.) You'll be immensely better for pushing through and persevering.
3.) It's an absolute necessity if you want to free yourself from the burden of your past.

Despite its necessity, most people can't seem to find their way free of the shackles of discontent. They remain the person that they were when they were married and never take the time to change the things about themselves that caused the divorce. Eventually, they find another spouse and the cycle of happiness, tragedy and divorce starts all over again.

This is the part of life that I want to talk about. It's something that I like to call "shedding the hell." You must be willing to stand up to your demons and say, "Enough is enough!"

If you have dreams and goals, you have to attack them daily but understand that it will require some change. You have to let the old you die. Divorce it and move forward.

The day you do decide to chase your dream, it will put you through some hell at first and for a long period of time, it may seem pointless. You must persist. These hard times will force you to change, using trials and everything possible to discourage you. Identify what they are and treat them as obstacles rather than sentences. Those who cannot, will find themselves lost all over again.

The people who are afraid and uncomfortable with change will give up and either find something new to pursue or settle. These people, who give up trying something new, will quickly find themselves faced with the same problems and in a different hell with the same devil—themselves.

This is because they didn't take the time to dig deep and shed their former selves completely, and just like the person who doesn't change about them what caused the divorce, they will make the same mistakes all over again and run into new trials and misfortunes. And again, they will be faced with the decision to divorce themselves and let the new them arise or continue "shedding the hell" until they smarten up and get to work. That's why some people are still in the same situations they've been in for years.

When divorcing yourself or in the process of changing, there will be times where the old you will try and pull you back into the depths of loss, anger, habits and confusion. This is inevitable, and it will happen but it doesn't have to happen. It's completely up to you. Agree to support your new self at all costs. Your very life and meaning depend on it.

Life is the opposing team and it wants you to fail. Remember that life is that selfish person who doesn't want to give you anything, but it knows it must relinquish everything to the person who perseveres, changes and keeps going—despite what they are faced with.

When those old habits come back knocking (and they will knock), that is the time to resist, pray and stand in courage. If you want to become who you dream of becoming, this is the only way.

Resistance, prayer, courage. This is, "easier said than done," but it's a must for your life and for your happiness. Don't pick flesh over FAITH.

This is also the time to do a thorough check of <u>what</u> in your life is causing you to slip backward in to your old ways. Isolate those things and excommunicate them from your day-to-day existence at any cost.

For instance, if you are trying to be a better husband and had issues with being faithful to your wife, then suddenly you are feeling the urge to cheat again, stop and look at what's causing these feelings. Are you flirting? Are you looking at porn? Are you on the social media sites where the women are half-dressed? Where have you gone astray? Acknowledge yourself and your weaknesses and that will make you stronger.

Take a full inventory of what's going on in your life that may be causing you to want to go back to old habits. Fight it and pray your way through it. This is a spiritual fight not a physical fight. The more you do this, the easier this process becomes and the closer you get to your destination.

Today, you attend your own funeral. Today, you lay your old ways to rest. Today is your first day of growth. Whatever it is; whether it's getting in shape, treating yourself better, being better with your finances, or self-control. Figure it out and change it. Change is terrifying but that's all it is. You have control over it, so do it the right way and stay the positive course.

No more repeating what caused you to fail you in the past. If you aspire to be a better person, you must do something different now or your next year will look like your last year.

Change you! Don't be afraid to change you, even if it disappoints the people around you. Don't try to change. Trying is glorified failure. No more trying. DO!

CHAPTER 7: WHAT IS YOUR PURPOSE?

What is your purpose? When you are very passionate about your life and don't know your purpose here on earth, everything, especially the things that don't matter, makes you angry. When there's no purpose, there's nothing to look forward to.

When I was going through a divorce, I found *my purpose. Understand that adversity introduces you to yourself.* The things that my ex-wife was doing to make me angry weren't bothering me as much but when I lost my purpose, I lost my focus. I became comfortable in my endless anguish. The things that she and I were going through began to eat at me.

I began to feel like that lost little boy again. He'd resurged, even though I'd convinced myself that I'd put him down for good. I was at war and made my ex-wife the face of my own self-destruction. I told myself that she was wishing for my downfall and without my purpose, it seemed like her wish would quickly be granted.

I stopped feeding the community. I stopped speaking at local schools. I stopped training the kids in my organization. Each morning prior to our burgeoning conflict, I would listen to motivational audios (Like Les Brown or Eric Thomas.)

During that period of my life, I'd acted as if I'd never learned any of the lessons that they'd preached; the very same lessons that had helped to propel me in that positive direction. I was broken, defeated, and in some sick way, I wanted to be there.

Life had bullied me into another corner and I'd forgotten how to fight my way back out. I was too consumed by my anger and frustration to see the truth beyond the blinding forest of my hatred. That little boy had returned with a vengeance that I never could have fathomed. I'd lost myself and I'd lost my purpose.

You have to search and look for your purpose. Every human being has a purpose. When a man or woman has no purpose in this world, you can bet that anger, resentment, destruction and frustration are close by.

We see it daily when we turn on the news and hear about people who are robbing banks and committing heinous crimes. Most likely, they never took the time to find their purpose and became so frustrated with their predicament that they allowed themselves to lose control. There's a danger in wandering and wanderers tend to remain that way. Find your purpose and fight for it.

All of us have the same amount of time in the day. The rich and the wealthy have just as many seconds, minutes and hours as the poor and poverty-stricken. Every minute of the day must be accounted for. Use that time to find your purpose. Your first step in becoming successful is first finding what you're meant to do.

You can't walk into your true greatness without first knowing your purpose. Once your purpose is found, the rest will swiftly follow.

I found my purpose in helping people. Motivating, teaching and assisting everyone that I could, in any way that I could, became my focus. I had a clear vision of what I wanted to do but I stopped working towards it. I stopped putting in that total effort.

I started to lose that vision and after my eyes were blurred I became frustrated, not just at myself but at everyone and everything around me.

I found myself sleeping in late, resting when I could have been putting that time towards my dream and allowing my mind to spiral into all manners of useless bullcrap. My vision suffered because I refused to see.

Keep your vision plain and destroy everything that threatens your dream and your ambition. Someone who is reading this may be is in a relationship that has taken you off course; you've lost your focus and your purpose. The thought of you leaving that person makes you feel bad so you convince yourself that it's not that bad and that person is for you. But take it from me, you will end up resenting that person and you will have internal issues that weren't there before you met that person. If being in that relationship threatens your destiny, it's time to be bold and move on, no condemnation. It takes a lot of hard work but there is no substitute for it. Roll up your sleeves and dig in the dirt for it, if you have to. Once you find your vision—your purpose—then the real work begins.

Now, you must figure out how to take this vision from your mind and bring it to fruition. This is when you have to be open to failure and roadblocks because this is when they will show up. This is also the time when you need to believe in yourself and create a tunnel for your dreams to pass through.

Life is designed to distract you. It's going to get tough when you decide to chase your dream. It's like robbing life of its treasures. Life is already selfish and it doesn't want to give you anything but the bare minimum. When you finally find your purpose, life gets angry and start to throw bills, problems, death, loss and a million other things in your path. That's its way of trying to knock you down. That's your sign to keep on pushing.

Life also knows that it's a double-edged sword. Never forget that those same things happening *to you* are also happening *for you.*

Whatever it is that may seem intent on tearing you down is the very same thing that will build you into the unstoppable force that you MUST become. If you don't pay attention to the blessings of struggle, failure and defeat, you will miss the lesson entirely.

"It doesn't matter what happened to you. What matters is <u>HOW YOU RESPOND TO IT!</u>"

Unfortunately, most people fail to see it this way but when you persevere and work hard every day towards your passion and your dream, life will stop fighting you and give in to you and your needs. It will hand over the keys to everything you've always dreamt about. All of this is possible.

No more sleeping in late, no more putting things off to take a nap, or rushing home to do nothing. You must work harder at <u>developing you.</u>

Instead of starting your day off by checking your social media, start your day off with prayer (no social media, no email, no text messages), then while you are brushing your teeth and washing your face—or whatever your morning routine is—listen to motivational audio or something informative that will educate and empower you.

Instead of surfing the web, look for classes that you can take. Invest in yourself. Take the time to make every day a little better than the one before it. Take minutes (or seconds, if you can't spare the time), to learn, experience and express. You are the painter and the canvas. Only you can decide how this all turns out and only you must walk with the results of it. PUT THE WORK IN TO YOU!

Today is your day! Never again will you give your least and allow life to just do what it wants to you. NO MORE EXCUSES. You are destined to be phenomenal! Your purpose is waiting to be found and to help you kick down barriers and doors that were meant to keep you stagnant.

Your purpose is your shield when life comes to knock you down. Dare to find out what you are made of! Stop quitting at the first signs of rejection and doubt. No more sitting there wishing and hoping.

Give yourself entirely to complete faith and action. Hope jumps off the edge <u>hoping</u> everything will be okay, faith jumps **knowing** everything will be okay.

Write down everything that you want in your life. Look at it every hour on the hour. Your purpose keeps you unstoppable. If you lose that vision, you're automatically weakened.

Remember, life is going to get hard as you get closer your dream. Don't quit. You may fall. You may hurt. You may cry. You may even want to throw in the towel, but you must fight through this and persist. You aren't the only one who's depending on you. Fight this life back. YOU CAN DO THIS!

Stop telling yourself that you don't deserve this dream and this life. You do and the only person who can talk you of your good life is you. If you want something different, you have to be different. Self-development is crucial.

When you find your purpose—and as you grow, your purpose will change—don't let it outgrow you. You have to be growing and preparing for the change in your purpose, because soon an opportunity will present itself and it will give you the chance to walk into your desired light.

It's better to be prepared and not have an opportunity then to have an opportunity and not be prepared. Yesterday is gone and tomorrow is too late. Sadly, when people are at the end of their lives, they usually regret the things they didn't do. Live fully, go out into the world and take chances and risks. If you feel you have multiple purposes, go after them all one by one. There is no reset button at the end of your life, this is it. No matter how old you are, you still have a purpose, only you can bring it to life. Take that step towards you dream that scares you to death. You MUST start TODAY!

CHAPTER 8: BELIEVE IN YOURSELF EVEN WHEN NO ONE DOES

The world is filled with people who are going to count you out, no matter how much you prove yourself. Your best will never be good enough for them. It doesn't matter how many times you've been knocked down or denied your dream. That doesn't matter. That's not the deciding factor.

The deciding factor is how many times you look up, get up and choose not to give up. I've learned that other people's opinion of you doesn't matter. It's not what people say about you that threatens your dreams and destination., it's what you say about you that ultimately destroys or decide your outcome.

Some people are so evil that they can't sleep well unless they hinder greatness and when those people see greatness, they immediately try to discourage it in the hopes of you viewing your talent and dreams the way they falsely view your talents and dreams. Make your dream so powerful—with massive action—that you can't be denied for long.

When you put massive action behind your dream by staying focused and striving for excellence, what can deny you? Not much. If you really want to get back at all the people who told you that you couldn't succeed and win and walk in your dream, get mad and get revenge. The best revenge? Massive success. That success is only possible through MONUMENTAL ACTION.

The first step to believing in yourself is to have a why. Why are you doing what you are doing? I had to do this part as well, but I had to dig deep. I couldn't just say, "my children are my why," although that's a great why. I had to dig deeper. God gave me my children as a reward for my success and my efforts but what moved me into action?

I was chasing my dream long before my children came into this world. I had to dig beneath it all. Beneath the gravel of my soul and the ice of my broken heart. I had to find what made me tick. I had to find my grand motivator.

After weeks and months of prodding the question in my mind, one day I just sat down and thought. I meditated on the question and after being completely honest with myself, I found out that my motivation was that I didn't want to repeat the history of my family. My grandfather is 73 and lives in a homeless shelter. I'm not judging him. I love him. One evening I asked him if there was anything he planned to leave behind if he ever died; a bold question but I wanted to know. His response was, "Nothing right now." I was floored. I said to myself, "He had 73 years to do whatever he wanted and he didn't even have $100 to leave to his grandchildren." Again, I'm not judging my grandfather but I had to find my why.

I love my family but no one created a life with anything worth leaving to the next generation. Prior to my brother and I, we were nothing but temporary sacks of flesh and blood—singing on faith and hoping without ever actually doing much in the way of progressing. Sad, but true. I would see people go to church on Sundays and would go back home to hell as if God was going to come down and give them a great life. No one took a risk and went out in the world and worked towards something to give God something to bless.

No one had life insurance. No one had real estate. No one owned a home. They spent their entire life making other people wealthy. No one had a career that we could look up to. No one traveled. No one had a college education. No one drove really nice cars. Their legacy was a bunch of broken homes and relationships and grudges held against family members. No one made a difference. Everybody was living check-to-check trying to survive the struggle and working just to pay bills. Everybody was existing and no one was living

Everyone would die and no one would ever know they were here because no one made a difference in this world. It's a brutal truth. It's a harsh reality. It's a very cold thing to hear and think about. But, at the end of the day, it's my truth and my grand motivator. I WILL leave something behind. People, even if it's only you, WILL know that I was here. They WILL know that I tried to make a difference.

So, I dare you to write down your dreams and goals and make it so plain that a third-grader can read it. After that, do the research. What do you have to do to become your dream? What books do you need to read? What classes do you have to take? What changes do you need to make? Nothing is more powerful than a mind that has decided to become better.

One of my dreams was to become a motivational speaker. I did my research. I joined Toastmasters. I paid for certification classes in life coaching to better understand people and to become one with people of all aspects of life. I stopped doing things that contradicted what I wanted to become.

I called middle schools and high schools to ask if I could go and speak to their students. I got as much practice as I possibly could. I refused to be denied. I reached out to my cousin, Terence Latham, who was successful and was also my motivator and I asked him question after question. He became my mentor and one day he gave me his formula, "Help people get what they want, you will get what you want." That's when I started my nonprofit helping kids and a food ministry where I feed hundreds of people every month.

I got information on starting my master's program in psychology. I wanted it more than I wanted to sleep, eat … anything. Like Eric Thomas says, "I wanted it more than I wanted to breathe." My "why" was stronger than anything in the world.

I tried even if I failed, because true failure in life is not trying at all. When you believe you are less than and worthless, you embody that feeling; meaning that everything you do on daily basis will result in that feeling of being worthless.

Quitting will take a toll on you and your self-worth. You will find yourself walking with your eyes on the ground. You will let people talk down to you and be okay with it. You will settle for mediocrity. You will settle for poor company. You will die inside.

If you embody that feeling of being powerful, smart and strong, you will walk with your head high and smiling from ear-to-ear. Your dreams will become clearer and people will treat you according to that embodiment. It will radiate off you like the smell of a good body wash.

Every day should be a personal development day for you. You can't go for days and weeks and not work out, because when you get back to the gym your muscles will be as sore as if you'd never done anything. The same goes for personal development and believing in yourself. Work your motivational muscles and hit THE PERSONAL DEVELOPMENT GYM.

Don't go for days and weeks and not develop you and your dreams, because after weeks and months without developing yourself, you will be drained and that small negative voice will come back stronger and begin to pull you back to where you fought so hard to get out of. You will start to settle for the status quo and it will get harder to get back on track.

This time is yours now—no more second-guessing yourself. Your dreams are possible. No one is built like you. Take life on. Say "yes" to your dreams. You can do this!

So what if people laugh at your dreams? Damn them. This is your time! You are possible! Go and do whatever it takes to accomplish your dreams. Do what is hard. Don't run from it. Face it straight on. Stand tall. Make it happen and dominate fear. If it's possible for me, it's possible for you.

Make today your first day of success and when the doubt and fear creep in, feel it and do it anyway. Keep belief in yourself no matter what, even if the picture in the frame looks impossible. Walk by faith, not by sight.

Sight will force you to quit but faith will have you looking at whatever is going on as a process that will have a great outcome.

The process is created to build a better you. I believe in you; believe in yourself. This time is yours. Remember, you aren't defeated by what people say about you and your dream, you are defeated by what <u>you</u> say about <u>you</u> and your dreams.

CHAPTER 9: WHAT DO YOU WANT?

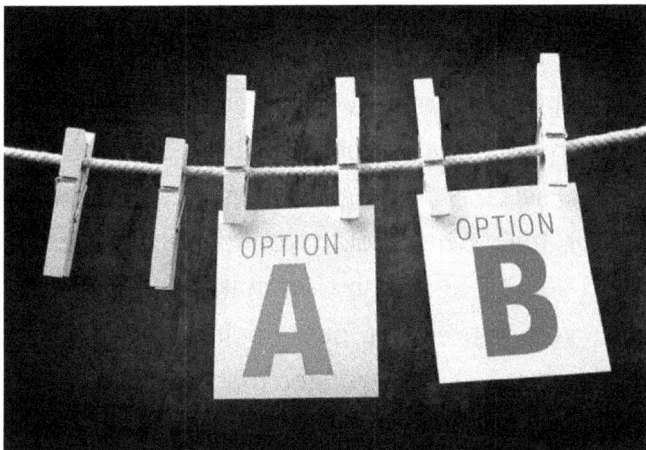

Life is full of negative people and events that have been designed to shut down dreams and life has created people who have settled for something that only pays their bills and barely keeps them fed. Even with their humdrum lives, so many people are scared pale at the thought of chasing their dreams. I ask ... WHY?! Your dreams are important and necessary.

The thought of losing your job and losing your comfort isn't the discouragement. You are! You have told yourself over and over that you can't do the things you dream of and that became your belief system. You are the one who determines the direction of your life.

Your belief system is not a fact. It's just your fear's opinion and I call bullshit. Excuse my language. God isn't done with me yet but I'm passionate about this. I came into this world with nothing and I want to leave this world and my children and family with everything. The only problem is, your doubt is stronger than your desire. Failure is not an option! What if you couldn't lose or fail? What would you do and how hard would you go at it, knowing that you couldn't fail? Once you figure that out, do it and make your hunger for success stronger than your comfort in starving. Your life will change immediately when you commit to change and chasing your dreams. Most people fantasize about their dream. Your dream doesn't have to be a fantasy; you just have to decide what you want out of your life. Stop accepting mediocrity and make the decision. What do you want?!

If you want something bad enough, dedicate yourself wholly to it and WORK! To be honest, today I am supposed to submit this book to my publisher. All day, the negative small talk has been whispering in my ear, "You aren't an author, Maurice." "You aren't good enough, Maurice." "It's not long enough, loser." "Who do you think you are?" "You grew up in poverty in public housing, you aren't an author." For a second, I listened. I allowed myself to feel the fear.

Because of that astronomical level of doubt and anxiety, I'd actually talked myself out doing one of the most important things that I'd ever do with my life and my profession. Because I let fear win, I stopped writing my book. That's right, this very one that you're reading now.

For a whole two months, I listened to fear's ugly voice and for a whole two months, I went without jotting down a single word—not even so much as a letter. On top of that, I was still making mistakes and I allowed that small voice to whisper in my ear, "How are you going to write a book and you made that mistake?" As the days turned into weeks, I found myself somehow even less confident than I had been in those initial paralytic moments.

I would look at my book, if only to add something, correct something, take something out (it's a hell of a process)—only to find that my fear and anxiety had built to such an extent that I couldn't even so much as string together a thought. I, a guy who desires to speak for a living, couldn't fathom a single word. At one point, it'd gotten so bad that I would literally be shaking over my keyboard. Do you see the power of fear?

So, what did I do? How did I overcome it? Well, that's easy. I took a page out of my own "book" (so to speak.) One day, after my ritualistic trembling, I got up and took a walk around the house. I took my scattered thoughts and washed them away with memories of how far I'd come.

I thought about that boy who missed his father. What would he say if he saw me like that? How would he feel to know that the man having a panic attack over a three-pound laptop was who he was to become? Then, it hit me. I don't have to ask. I don't even have to know. All that I had to do was *ACT.*

"One word at a time," I told myself "Just one." I had to address the problem. Just like most times, it was *me* again. It was time for a change.

That night, instead of stressing out over the computer, I just had a snack and laid in bed, repeated affirmations and relaxed my mind until I fell asleep. I asked myself, "What do you want to be remembered for, Maurice? Who do you want to be this time next year?" I slept for two hours and got up and started writing. I had to push through the struggle and the fear, but I knew I had to do this for me. I wanted to separate myself from what I knew—growing up with courage and character. I wanted to be great and I knew greatness doesn't come from sleeping. I knew that every decision mattered. I may have still had the fear but I knew how to throw it off.

Fear likes to latch itself to certain constants to keep it breathing and fed. To jolt yourself out of it, the best thing to do, is to change the habit that your fear is feeding from. My solution was to write in the morning; early enough that I could focus and late enough that I would be well-rested and clear-minded.

After only sleeping for two hours I got up and I wrote more in a handful of hours than I had in the six-months prior. I disconnected with my fear. The entire time my head kept shaking up and down lightly as if I was saying "yes" to something and I was! I was giving myself permission to do what most people fear—write a book. I didn't care how I looked at the moment—just like you have to do when chasing your dream—you will look crazy to other people when you are doing something they were afraid to do and I didn't run from it. I identified its source. It found me in the dark and feasted on my doubt.

By dragging that fear into the light, for all to see, I forced my fear to reckon with the fact that I am more powerful than it tells me. I am greater than the sum of my doubt. So are you. No matter who you are or what you've done. You can beat it, too. I'm beating it right now.

YOU'RE BEATING IT RIGHT NOW!

I know that the only person who can stop me from writing this book, is me. This is what I want to do and I'm doing it.

As a kid who grew up poor, survived on government assistance, lived public housing, was counted out at birth, fatherless, the first to graduate high school and college, play professional basketball ... it was hell, But from that hell, I rose clean and brand-spanking new. By the grace of God, I've arrived as I am today.

Now I have a great job, my own business, am in the process of purchasing a home for my family and about to submit my first book to a big-time publisher.

If I can do this, so can you. I don't care how old you are. You still have dreams, goals and ideas. Bring them out and find a way to accomplish them and no matter how hard it gets—even when you can't see it—you have to keep going. Keep pushing. Saying one "no" to your dream can cost you years of progress. It's not easy but never give up!

The time of being blind and living as if there is a reset button is done. Your life as you know it is over, ITS TIME TO WORK! The time for the greatest test that you will ever take IS NOW! Will you quit when your vision is blurred, or will you continue to fight for your right to dream and see them come true?

A lot of people wake up energized and motivated and a few hours later they're back to the normal, "I'm tired of these people," "I hate my job," etc. The reason for this has to do with one's habits.

See, most people get up and nourish their bodies: Wash their face, brush their teeth, and eat a delicious breakfast to jump start their day and go out into a negative world where there are negative people and others who can't wait to ruffle some feathers and ruin their day.

The direction of your life has to change and it is determined by you. Those things don't matter anymore. Those people don't matter anymore. All that matters are you, your loved ones, and WHAT YOU NEED TO ACHIEVE.

Stop living life like an accident and make the first minute of every day your time to fine- tune your brain and thoughts. The first twenty minutes of the day are the most influential minutes. Don't waste them!

If you look at the news and its negativity, you will unknowingly and subconsciously attract more negativity throughout the day. When the negative people you already have to deal with reverse what you put inside yourself come together, it will frustrate you to the core. It will haunt you like a wicked ghost. It will penetrate your hope and dash your motivation. THIS CAN NOT BE YOU ANYMORE!

Create positive habits and make a decision to be great. Fix what is mediocre and change your routine.

Instead of listening to the negative news, listen to motivational tapes and read inspirational books to start your day. Instead of hopping out of bed and starting your day with email or a social media scroll, meditate and take a moment to be grateful for what you have. Instead of eating that donut or pancake for breakfast, try fruit or oatmeal and a peaceful stroll around the block.

The key here is to start every day off with a large heaping dose of positivity and clarity of self. Your problems will present themselves. You must search for your solutions. That only comes with time, patience and maximum effort. Be committed to that and hold yourself accountable. Set an alarm. Write it down. Say it out loud. Do WHATEVER you have to do to follow through.

Remember, what doesn't get better gets worse. A man or woman without a vision and a dream will perish along with their stagnancy.

CHAPTER 10: STOP TALKING YOURSELF OUT OF GREATNESS

Imagine this if you will ... At birth, and I'm talking about everybody in this world who was born without any birth defects, (but even with birth defects I've seen people do the impossible), but when everyone was born, I believe that God gave everyone their own personal gift, dream and vision. Along with those things, he gave us our own personal "ladder of success" and said, "I give you free will. It's up to you to climb this ladder."

A rare few people start out taking that first step, second step and eventually they make it to the top of the ladder and enjoy the life God wants us to enjoy. More people take a few steps, get comfortable and stay there because they're too afraid to rock the boat and take chances, so they settle and talk themselves into believing they're content with where they're at.

Then, you have MOST people who take the first couple steps and then life starts to happen. A few failures, heartbreaks and missteps scare them off the ladder. They take steps back down to where it was comfortable and safe. I believe that such people were the ones who coined the old saying, "Every time I take two steps forward, I take ten steps back."

Finally, you have people who've never even taken the first step and blame the world, society and all other manner of things, for their poor circumstances and their lack of spirit and ambition. These people may as well have never been given a ladder at all.

Even with all of their gifts and opportunities, they never take that first step because they've missed out on one crucial idea. There is no one to blame for your lack of success, but you.

God has done the best that he could with you. Everything you need to be successful you already have inside of you. Society has done the best that it could with you. Your parents have done the best that they could for you. The only person not putting in the effort to help you out, is YOU!

How dare you blame everything and everyone else for your own fear to act! How dare you curse your creator's name while you lay stagnant. How dare you breathe another lazy breath about what someone else is doing. If you're this person, you should be ashamed of yourself. If you're not, let this be my warning to you: DO NOT BE THAT PERSON.

That person doesn't want success. That person only wants to drag you down to hell right beside them, just so that they could tell you how bad you are. DON'T BE THIS PERSON. Don't fall into the trap of being the "victim." You can't be a victim. I won't allow you to be a victim. God did not put you here to be a victim.

You are the creator of your life. God gave you life and left it up to you to create something out of it. What you have in your life YOU created. What you don't have in your life, you've talked yourself out of. Whatever you have done and thought about up to this point in your life, it is working, whether good or bad.

An insurmountable percentage of your greatness is determined by your own self-talk. Your self-talk ignites your greatness or smothers it. Again, this is your decision and there's no one to blame for your own negative self-talk, but YOU! Point the finger at YOU! You are the author and your life is a movie. The good thing is, you are the director and you have the power to take out scenes you don't like and replace them with better ones. You have to power to yell "cut" when things are going as planned and you have the power to start all over again. I want you to read the next few paragraphs aloud, make It personal.

Dear ME. Why aren't I where I should be? Your intentions are good but why do you start your day off with clicking a button, dimming your light on your phone and squinting your eyes to check on other people's lives? There you go putting your dreams second again!

How long before you focus on your dreams? DAMN IT! How long will you focus on what you don't want? Don't you know whatever you think about long enough will manifest? How long will you continue to talk yourself out of your own greatness? How long will you be afraid to be you, not caring what other people think about you? You're always saying it's too hard or speaking other useless negativity into existence. Come on, man!

The more you tell yourself you "can't" or it's "hard," the more there's a need to check your surroundings. Something is reaching your heart, coming out of your mouth, manifesting in your words and your dreams are falling far behind.

See, you expect a different result, something like success but you continue to be the same person you were years ago; afraid to stand up for your dreams ... playing life backwards, cheating on your spouse, gambling away all of your money, drinking yourself into debt. Then you want to get on your knees and pray for that great life. You tell me. Where's the sense in that? As the chocolate bar says, "Give me a break!"

You've been with you for decades, so no annulment. Sorry, it's too late for that. But a divorce is your best bet. Come up and get your clean slate.

Yesterday is gone but the people from your past will try to remind you of who you once were. Be aware. Put your middle finger up to your old ways. You can't create anything beautiful tomorrow by doing the same ugliness that you were doing last week.

Your dreams have been sidelined for years with its Nikes on, headband tight and one helluva shot; ready to get the game.

But you, the coach, never called his name because you let laziness be your point guard, procrastination be your center, envy run the team, jealousy control your lane and hate dominate the game. That's your starting five? You're letting them play all forty-eight minutes? You must be out of your damn mind!

If I saw that, I wouldn't even bother watching you lose. I'd just look at your bench and apologize for how bad their coach was.

Why play the trash, when you've got a bench full of SUPERSTARS? Ambition's hungry for its time. Drive's pissed off and ready for success. Will's itching to get a shot. Perseverance is hollering your name. Greatness is waiting for you to call on him, so he can get in the game and SHOW YOU what makes him so GREAT!

These are THE KINGS, coming second and you wonder why you don't have a ring!

Why are we this way?

Who did this to us?

What did this to us?

It doesn't matter anymore. All that matters is this:

YOU ARE WORTH ALL YOUR EFFORT. YOU ARE POWERFUL. YOUR BIGGEST CHALLENGE IN LIFE IS YOU. BE RELENTLESS AND REFUSE TO BE DENIED. GO TO YOUR GRAVE BROKE WITH NOTHING LEFT. DON'T JOIN THE PEOPLE WHO DIED WITH SO MUCH POTENTIAL; MILLION DOLLAR IDEAS, UNWRITTEN BOOKS AND SONGS THAT WAS SUPPOSED TO CHANGE LIVES. DON'T DIE WITH THAT GIFT THAT WAS GIVEN TO YOU STILL INSIDE.

DON'T REJECT YOUR LADDER!

CHAPTER 11: DEALING WITH THE ISSUE OF FORGIVENESS

If there is one thing in your control that can hold you back from achieving your greatness and living your dreams, it's the lack of forgiveness. Holding onto hatred, no matter how miniscule, is the most potent way to derail yourself from the track of success and all of the good things that success will bring you.

When I was going through my divorce, two years after being legally separated, I'd finally found the strength to move on.

I couldn't do it alone, mind you. As he does, God blessed me with exactly what he knew I needed while showing me the exact type of woman

NOT to seek. I'd gotten out of that toxic relationship and afterward met Victoria Dent, a breath of fresh air.

Life, however, had different plans for me, (or maybe it was just a test.) Victoria and I had only been talking and hanging out for about a year. She knew that I needed to take things slow and that I was still somewhat recovering from an ugly situation at the time. She stuck by my side through my divorce—and all of the subsequent, drama, arguments, attacks and teardowns.

Finally, the day had come on January 9, when all of the drama would come to an official end. The divorce was already finalized and I could at last, move on with my life. Despite all of that, there was a part that could not let go.

The horror show was going to be over, but I'd still been torn up inside. My inner voice loved the suffering. I was used to it. Anything other than that frightened the hell out of me. The emotional surgery was over, but I'd still been a deep pain.

One night after replaying in my mind that the life I once knew was over, I found myself unable to sleep. I sat up at the edge of the bed and cycled through all of the awful things that had happened in my life and wondered what the point of any of it ever was.

I had been allowing my inner voice to torment and have its way with me. My hatred boiled but in the midst of my downward spiral, Victoria got up and stood in front of me between my legs, wrapped her arms around me and squeezed as tightly as she could.

I told her how much pain that I was in. I barely remember the moment; I'd been spilling my soul so freely. She just held me tighter and told me that, "Everything will be okay. It's okay to let it out." In that moment, stubborn old Maurice finally crumbled. Tears ran down my face like they'd been building up for decades.

It was an endless stream that represented a lifetime of anger and frustration. From my father leaving, my stepfather's abuse, my mother's cancer, my sister's death, my lost dream of going pro, my torn ACL and my broken home. It all came out in that moment. Just as soon as each tear hit the mattress, the pain left right along with it.

All of my anger and hatred washed away and was replaced with the only thing in my life that mattered. Happiness. My own, my family's, Victoria's and all of those out there in the world whom I could help. I let go of the negativity and was reborn as the man that I'd always told myself that I was. I forgave my pain. Then, I forgave myself.

Victoria, that night you saved my life. I am endlessly indebted to your kindness, love and grace. I love you more than words could tell, mouths could speak, and hearts could bleed. You are my life, my love, my everything.

Side Note:

For those of you reading this, who may not want to wait for this type of breakdown (and you shouldn't let it go on long enough that you do), may I recommend reaching out to a loved one and allowing them into your soul, just long enough for them to see who you TRULY are.

Let them see you for what burdens you. Let them see your truth. Let them tell you that it's okay to be that person. It *IS* okay to be that person. That's the person that you need to be to be free.

Should you not have someone like that in your life, may I suggest that you take your truth to whatever Higher Power that you subscribe to. Go to them with this prayer:

"God,
Grant me the serenity, to accept the things I cannot change, the courage to change the things I can, and the wisdom to know the difference."

Afterward, you let go. Let go of the hatred. Let go of the blame. Let go of all of those things that haunt you when the lights go out and all that you're left with is your thoughts. Let go of them and fill the void with love, empathy and a commitment to being better.

***

After I'd finally gotten my bearings back, I realized that I was still angry. I was still in pain. Not the same pain that I'd felt as a boy, but a flesh wound that my inner voice had hoped I would let fester and rot. For a moment there was a time where I'd thought of shutting down. My hopes, my dreams, everything. All that I wanted was revenge.

For more time than I could remember, I would sit up late at night thinking about how much I'd despised my ex-wife. How for years I begged her for love and affection and she refused. Thoughts of her were like a dim light that sprang up in mind whenever I couldn't find something else to distract me from the pain I'd felt.

My loathing of her boiled inside of me like a pan of hot grease over a fire. All that I could think about was her "being against me," and "trying to take me down." It was like I was back in college all over again. Only this time—the enemy had gotten in.

I felt vulnerable, betrayed and weak. All the while I was marinating in my emotions. I felt my hopes and dreams begin to drift further and further away from me.

As any divorcee with kids would tell you, that part of the process was particularly damaging—not only to the kids but to myself—and I imagine my ex-wife, as well. We'd spent too long in a situation that just wasn't working. Now, I was paying the price.

The legal intervention and the hateful back and forth that we'd shared with one another was draining. I hate to admit it, but for a while there, I lost sight of my goals. I lost sight of who I was. Now, a grown man, I'd again shifted away from who I was and had lost touch with my identity. Even my new girlfriend and I suffered a strain in our relationship. Suddenly, I was losing again and I couldn't figure out why.

I dropped to my knees in prayer—as I do whenever things get tough—and I asked God to take away the pain or show me how to crawl my way out of it. Then, like some sort of lightning bolt, it hit me. My own lesson. I was the problem.

Yes, my hatred gave me some temporary relief and an ability to vent my frustration, but what was it really doing? What was I gaining? Who was I becoming? The answer to all three questions is the same. Nothing. All it did was lengthen the distance between me and my dreams

If I wanted to keep what I'd gained in my success, I had to let go of the hatred in my heart. I had to forgive my ex-wife and more importantly, I had to forgive myself for the time that I'd wasted being angry with her. Sometimes, the only way to hold on, is to let go.

I didn't want my life and my beautiful new girlfriend to be cheated because of my unwillingness to forgive. I didn't want myself to drown in the long pit of doom that is resentment toward another person. Life is a bully enough already, *"Why am I helping a bully?"* I thought.

Just like that, I was back on track and free of the weight that I'd forced myself to carry for all those months. I was me again. Thankfully, I didn't wander off too far.

So, I ask you now, who aren't you forgiving? Who still takes up real estate in your mind that they didn't pay for? Who haven't you reached out to; to express your condolences for their sadness? When will you forgive yourself for the time that YOU'VE wasted? In order for you to truly become what and who you envision when you close your eyes, forgiveness must lead your life.

I urge you to clean up your side of the metaphorical street. DO IT TODAY! DO IT NOW! Save the page and go handle your business! Remember, it's not just for them but for you as well.

When you don't forgive and subsequently allow yourself to hold resentment against someone, you are wasting not only your time, but God's time. He put that ladder there for you, remember? Why would you insult him by going over to kick someone off theirs? Even so, it's not your primary concern. YOU'VE GOT A DREAM TO CHASE. Life won't stop just because you've got an attitude or a broken heart or hurt feelings. The sun still rises and you've still got a world to conquer.

For a long time, I hated my ex-wife but at the same time I wanted to become a great man. That didn't mix well. I suffered because every relationship that I became a part of—whether business or personal—I destroyed unintentionally but I destroyed them. This happened because I was operating with those strong hateful emotions that I allowed myself to have.

My hatred for my ex-wife caused me to be impatient, intolerable, snappy, mean and downright nasty. At first, it was in the form of a light switch. I could turn those bad emotions off when I wanted to and when I saw her or talked to her, the switch would flip right back on.

The more I let that resentment sit, the more those bad emotions and habits became who I was. And soon enough, the switch was on permanently and my life started to unravel at the seams. Everyone had become my enemy again.

I'd convinced myself over and over that I forgave her but then I came to the realization that when your affirmations aren't working, and it seems as if everything you are trying isn't working, that's an indication that there's some forgiving that's been left undone.

Holding on to the past will always keep you held prisoner to it. We must let go and forgive completely.

There are two methods of doing this. They are forgiving and acceptance of it. When you forgive, you can leave it at that and spin around in your mind when you find that the anger still lingers. That's the way that most people do it. For most people, I guess that's fine.

However, when you forgive AND accept it, you've allowed your heart to free itself of even the smallest thought of the wrong that was done to you. You release all negative energy and thought of the person or event and you move on and forward with your life.

Learn to forgive but, just as importantly, learn to accept that you've forgiven. You'll be better for it and the other person will as well, (whether or not that's your intent.) It's always better to keep the negativity to a minimum, the joy to a maximum, and the vision at 100%.

Forgive yourself. Forgive them. Accept it. Move on.

CHAPTER 12: MOVE FORWARD - YOUR LIFE DEPENDS ON IT

Everything that has happened to you, the people that have hurt you, the things that have traumatized you, or whatever other negative thing that you carry with you each day—you have to forgive in order to thrive and move forward. If you allow bitterness to live in your head and heart, your life will suffer and you will suffer. Let it go. The past has to die. Don't let your past failures and pain redefine you.

If you allow your mind to dwell in the past and allow your heart to hate, it will change your name from your birth name to "Bitter," "Hateful," "Mean," or "Ugly." Use today to reclaim your name. Use this time to renew your mind. Make today the first day of the rest of your life.

Your future is depending entirely on you being able to forgive your past. It takes courage, but if you've gotten this far, I believe that you've got what it takes. You can't walk into your future still thinking in your past. Don't let the pain win this battle. Save your mind—no more suffering. You will suffer if you don't forgive your past. AM I CLEAR?!

Whoever it is who has hurt you—no matter what they have done to you—call them now. I dare you to speak the words, "I forgive you." If you have hurt someone, I dare you to call them and ask them for forgiveness.

Growing and forgiving goes in order, just like a car. You don't just get in your car and start driving, do you? No. There's a process to it. Like everything else.

You must first get in the car. That's taking the first step and deciding to forgive.

Next you close the door. That's committing to your forgiveness.

After that, you put on your seat belt. No turning back. Say it with me. "I AM FORGIVING." The road may get bumpy but you've already committed.

Then, you check your mirrors, the sides and the rear view. This is the last time that you will ever look back at what's hurt you.

Now, start the car. Call or meet with the person.

Finally, you put the car in drive. Take the leap. Have faith. And, no matter what, maintain your promise to LET IT GO.

Trust me. This will take you some time but it will be so worth it in the end. This forgiveness is not for them, it's for you. Do your work. Forgive and move forward. Your dreams are being held back because of your inability to forgive. You can't change the past; just give your very best right now and every day for a better existence.

When you hold on to your pain, you are giving that person your power and energy and it's draining you daily. Don't even give that person your attention if forgiveness isn't an option. Do whatever you have to do after you forgive them and move on. Whether it's blocking them on social media, changing your number or taking a different route to work. Whatever it takes. GET THE NEGATIVITY OUT OF YOUR LIFE BUT MAKE SURE YOU FORGIVE THEM.

This is your life and you only get one chance to live it. Don't allow your past to keep you in the passenger seat. Don't be a victim this time. Let that pain push you to be better.

Don't go another day living in that misery. Focus on you. Focus on the things that you wish to accomplish. Keep your goals in front of all of those negative things that threaten to knock you off of the positive path that you've created for yourself.

Remember that we are all just people and that their word is only as good to you or as bad to you as you allow it to be. Maintain your power. Protect your happiness. You are more than what the hateful people know you are. But, it's not your job to tell them that.

Understand that those people are miserable inside and because of their misery, they have the incessant urge to spread it around and infect as many happy people as they can. It's what they do because, "hurt people, *hurt* people." Words to live by. A lesson to remember.

CHAPTER 13: FRIENDS TO FOES

When you decide to chase something bigger than yourself, some of the people closest to you may begin to dislike you and hate you. You are human, so this will bother you. People will make you feel as if what you are chasing is wrong. Some people will even try to shatter your name in hopes of getting people to see you in a different light, a negative one.

This is when you put your head down and believe in yourself. This is when you don't let those negative comments affect you. This is when you use the negativity to feed your actions. This is when you perfect self-control and your emotions. Don't react to them but react to your dreams.

Daily, you get better, get up earlier, pray, write your dreams down and go to work immediately on improving yourself mentally because your thoughts creates your life. If you aren't mentally powerful, you can't be physically prepared.

During this storm, you have to find a higher power. In my case, it's Christ. When you finally decide to play on a higher scale, life will fight against you. When you change your thoughts and activate the beast inside of you, life will come for you.

Life is going to happen. Don't let life have you just existing, don't settle for a mediocre life. God didnt create you to live a mediocre life. Keep your dreams and goals clear, even if it doesn't look as if you are getting anything done. Keep working. Keep setting goals.

You will have to fight against life and adversity. Don't stop at failure. Know the difference between failure and temporary setbacks.

Failure is completely giving up when you hit the water. When you are chasing your dream, you will fall in the water. You don't drown and fail unless you stay there.

Temporary setbacks are just that ... temporary and it's completely up to you for how long that lasts.

In taking the risk to accomplish your dreams, you will be faced with both of these things. You can look at this in many different ways but I choose to look at them as opportunities that will allow me to get closer to my dream. Every setback gets me closer to my destination.

At times, you will feel as if you are on an island alone and it will seem as if some of the people who you thought cared the most about you are against you. ITS TRUE! As it is with all forms of success, the further you go up the ladder of success, the more they want to see you fall. Persevere beyond it.

I can recall one time when I wasted my time with someone who I thought had my best interest at heart. During this argument, the person's real feelings emerged and they told me boldly to my face, "I can't wait to see you fall on your face."

It hurt, but it was humbling. It taught me that not everyone evolves and progresses, just because I have and that not everyone will remain the same as I change. It was a harsh reality (as many are), but it reminded me to stay vigilant, stay focused, stay positive, and most of all, stay aware of my surroundings. Stay aware of my bubble of trust. And if need be, be prepared to do it solo.

You must be willing to stand alone with just you and your dreams. Every day there has to be work done towards your dream and personal development. Some of your own family and friends may even be waiting and watching to see if you will prove them right. Don't let their limits limit you. You can do this.

Find opportunities in your day to work on you. If it's in traffic and someone cuts you off, use that to work on patience and kindness. If your ex-spouse tries to get you to lose your cool because they know your weaknesses, use this as a chance to be unbothered and a chance to work on not reacting but being in control of your emotions. If anything happens that runs the risk of throwing you off your game, find the lesson in it.

Don't give your enemies and haters the opportunity to say, "I told you so." Work so hard at your dream and force them to say. "I hate them even more." No, I'm not saying live to make your haters mad or prove them wrong, well actually I am. I want you to piss those F%$# off even more by relentlessly going after your dreams and what the world said you couldn't have. Use your haters as a driving force. Don't lose yourself in your situation. Don't forget who you are. Always take five minutes a day to appreciate how far you've come.

If you are in a situation right now where you feel the world is against you, keep going, keep striving, stay consistent and keep working. The adversity is temporary; it only becomes permanent if you stop striving. The life you want is possible. The car you want to drive is possible. The home you want to live in is possible. Keep working towards your dreams daily and let the haters hate.

CHAPTER 14: THE LITTLE BOY THAT DIED

They say you can have all the faith in the world, but if you don't give God something to bless, you are just a volunteer victim if things don't work out. I had some issues that were going on inside of me that I desperately wanted to deal with. I avoided them for years and they would show up when I was faced with some type (any type) of adversity.

I was physically a man but inside was a boy reacting on raw emotion and feeding on my own negativity. In my mind, I was nothing more than the same messed-up kid who escorted my soul into the dark abyss that I'd fought so hard to get out of. The scariest part of it all, was that I no idea.

I remember when my coach Emory Addison told me that I was a "man's man." I didn't understand that then. I didn't see myself as much more than a victim of my own circumstances. Powerless. If only he'd known just how wrong he was.

I was a grieving child trapped inside of a man's body and hoping that the pain would stop. When it didn't, I'd inflict it on others to numb myself. Like a toddler or a pre-teen, I'd throw tantrums, show my strength by breaking things, curse like I was never taught better, etc.

To discover that—even with all of my progress—that boy was still there was disheartening. I knew that I had to take action. I had to, if I wanted to keep the things that I'd earned and prevent myself from returning to that hellish pit of self.

I wanted to become more but I knew that to change my situation I had to change me first. So, I faced myself in the mirror and I was brutally honest with who I was and the things that were wrong with me. I started with the boy.

What did I need to do to put the boy in me to rest? I realized that I was still hurting from my childhood. I was resisting and avoiding dealing with not having a dad. I'd bandaged it up instead of healing it. I lost a lot of time running from my truth instead of just being honest with myself.

You may have the same issue, or an entirely different one, but the principle remains the same. You must put that little girl or little boy to rest so that the powerful you can take his or her rightful place at the wheel. Be honest with yourself and face what hurt you and deal with it.

I decided that I would give God something to bless and instead of blaming my dad and being angry with him (and he had no idea I was angry), I took the necessary steps to fix it.

I simply searched for him. That was the first step in healing and the first step in putting that boy to rest. I gave GOD something to bless.

In my search, Victoria recommended that I do one of those Ancestry DNA tests that have become quite popular. I took the test and after about a six-week wait, it came back with a list of people who may have been possible matches for my family members. The highest percentage match was a woman by the name of Katara Wright.

Mind you, I'd still been a bit skeptical about the whole thing. I was persistent in finding my father but I was never raised to trust much that resulted from the "digital age." Even still, I decided that I would send her message. After about two weeks passed without a reply, I moved on to the next closest match, Fran.

Fran and I talked for days, trying to put together our respective halves of a story that had been a relative (no pun intended) mystery to the both of us. She informed me that a cousin of hers had given birth to two sons. One of them was named John. *John* was my father's name.

All the air escaped from my body as my heart pounded against the inside of my chest. Fran asked me if I would like her to ask him to contact me. After a desperate pause, I agreed.

A few days after that, I was awoken by a *"bing"* sound on my phone—a *Facebook* notification. It was three in the morning and I'd had a particularly long day. Usually, I would just turn my phone off and return to sleep but *something* told me to look.

To my complete and utter surprise, I saw that a man by the name of John Wright had liked one of my photos. I clicked on his profile. *"IT WAS HIM!"* I thought. Needless to say, I didn't get much sleep that night. My mind was a swirl of hope and possibility.

The next day, he called me to arrange a date when the two of us could meet. It wasn't anything epochal but it was the first step toward a major missing piece of my life. Finally! An answer! *THE*

ANSWER!

On June 23, the two of us met at a hotel about midway between my home and where he'd been staying. I rushed to his hotel door—trying to look cool while doing so (I know that I didn't.) I knocked on the door and seconds later there he was. At 32, I was standing face-to-face with a man who looked like an older me. A man who didn't know I loved him more than any man in the world, A man who didn't know he was my hero because of my mother's words about him.

He smiled and invited me in. We spoke for a while (a bit defensive, understandably.) As we kept on in our conversation and shared knowledge of our past, our tempers eased and all that we'd known had seemed to line up perfectly. We spent the rest of the day in each other's company. It was the closest that I'd ever let a man get to me without courting a fight.

The next day, he agreed to the DNA test and we parted ways. At that point, I didn't really need it. At best, he was my dad. At worst, I knew that even if he wasn't, finding him was possible, as long as I kept pushing and fighting. Though, I really hoped that he was.

When the test came back I was at the movie theater. It was a 99.999% percent match. When I got the results, I had to hold back the tears to keep myself from looking crazy in the movie theater. I was at a complete loss for words.

The only thing that I could feel was gratitude and the unexplainable feeling of that last chain—that tethered me to my past—snapping loose and releasing me out into the world as I would then choose to make it.

I hugged my father. I thanked him for being there. No matter of the years that he missed; that moment was all it took to erase the void deep within me. I was free. I was whole. I was Maurice Latham-WRIGHT! The long search for my identity had finally come to close. That little boy who'd been haunting me for all those years—my inner voice— picked out a casket.

I went to New York and was accepted by my father and his family. He apologized for missing the first 33 years of my life and he promised me that he wouldn't miss any more. The little boy in me was buried.

The man arrived. I arrived. The way I dealt with men and people from that day forward changed. I no longer keep men who wanted to befriend me away. I no longer allowed my mind to convince me that people had bad intentions. I enjoy the time that I spend with friends, rather than scrutinize their presence. I welcomed people.

When my girlfriend and I would have disagreements, in the past, I would say "forget it" and stay quiet. After the boy died and we had disagreements, I would grab her and comfort her and kiss her to make her smile. I was no longer operating from a boy's standpoint. I was finally a man driving my life and making decisions. I didn't have to worry about losing any more. I was finally able to accept that I'd won.

If you are hurting and still healing from childhood wounds, it's time to look yourself in the mirror and be completely honest with yourself. What's hurting you? What are you avoiding? What are you not dealing with?

Face that hurt. You can't grow if you allow the past hurt to drive. You can't drive a car to your destination if your hands are tied behind your back. But if you face the situation, if you're honest with yourself and deal with it, it will free you and the new you will arrive.

Like you _must_ now do, I had to be honest with myself. I had to tell myself the truth. It's not only important for those people whom you may interact with, but for yourself.

I told myself all the things that I'd known to be true and what the world saw when they looked my way. I had to dig up the bones and skeletons of my past and bury them properly.

I told myself:

"Yes, you are a liar and a cheater."

"Yes, you are selfish."

"No, you're not perfect."

"No, you're not hopeless."

"He hurt me, but I must forgive him"

"You need to get better to be better."

I faced my demons instead of acting as if they never existed. I force-fed myself reality. I picked up books and absorbed whatever help that I could find. I invested in myself so that I could become the man that I am today.

It sounds simple, and the first step is the hardest. Despite the difficulty, you'll find that honesty with yourself *IS* the beginning of your journey back to you and the foundation for the greatness that you will become.

What aren't you dealing with? Deal with it. Your future depends on it. If you want your next five years to be better than your last five years, you must face you.

You are your greatest enemy. That little boy or that little girl will no longer be in control of your emotions and your decisions. Today, you will deal with it even if it means confronting what hurt you, even if it gets a little ugly. The butterfly only happens after an ugly worm emerges from an ugly cocoon. Use your pain. Grow from your cocoon of anguish. Dare to live!

You can do this. Go confront your little boy and girl and receive your new life. Today marks the day of the new you. You are done with the distractions and are on your way to your destination. Live! Learn! Love! Succeed!

You deserve it.

Take care.

—*Maurice*